A Note From Rick Renner

I am on a personal quest to see a "revival of the Bible" so people can establish their lives on a firm foundation that will stand strong and endure the test when the end-time storm winds begin to intensify.

In order to experience a revival of the Bible in your personal life, it is important to take time each day to read, receive, and apply its truths to your life. James tells us that if we will continue in the perfect law of liberty — refusing to be forgetful hearers but determined to be doers — we will be blessed in our ways. As you watch or listen to the programs in this series and work through this corresponding study guide, I trust that you will search the Scriptures and allow the Holy Spirit to help you hear something new from God's Word that applies specifically to your life. I encourage you to be a doer of the Word that He reveals to you. Whatever the cost, I assure you — it will be worth it.

> Thy words were found, and I did eat them;
> and thy word was unto me the joy and rejoicing of mine heart:
> for I am called by thy name, O Lord God of hosts.
> — Jeremiah 15:16

Your brother and friend in Jesus Christ,

Rick Renner

Resisting Evil

Copyright © 2018 by Rick Renner
8316 E. 73rd St.
Tulsa, Oklahoma 74133

Published by Rick Renner Ministries
www.renner.org

ISBN 13: 978-1-68031-594-3

eBook ISBN 13: 978-1-68031-632-2

How To Use This Study Guide

This five-lesson study guide corresponds to *"Resisting Evil" With Rick Renner* (RENNER TV). Each lesson in this study guide covers a subject that is addressed during the program series, with questions and references supplied to draw you deeper into your own private study on this subject.

To derive the most benefit from this study guide, consider the following:

First, watch or listen to the program prior to working through the corresponding lesson in this guide. (Programs can also be viewed at **renner.org** by clicking on the Media/Archives links.)

Second, take the time to look up the scriptures included in each lesson. Prayerfully consider their application to your own life.

Third, use a journal or notebook to make note of your answers to each lesson's Study Questions and Practical Application challenges.

Fourth, invest specific time in prayer and in the Word of God to consult with the Holy Spirit. Write down the scriptures or insights He reveals to you to be more effective personally in resisting things that are not of God.

Finally, take action! Whatever the Lord tells you to do according to His Word, do it.

For added insights on this subject, it is recommended that you obtain Rick Renner's CD series **Resisting the Enemy.** You may also select from Rick's other available resources, including his book *Spiritual Weapons To Defeat the Enemy,* by placing your order at **renner.org** or by calling 1-800-742-5593.

TOPIC

Resisting Temptation

SCRIPTURES

1. **1 Corinthians 10:13, 14** — There hath no temptation taken you but such as is common to man: but God is faithful, who will not suffer you to be tempted above that ye are able; but will with the temptation also make a way to escape, that ye may be able to bear it. Wherefore, my dearly beloved, flee from idolatry.

2. **1 Corinthians 10:19, 20** — What say I then? That the idol is any thing, or that which is offered in sacrifice to idols is any thing? But I say, that the things which the Gentiles sacrifice, they sacrifice to devils, and not to God: and I would not that ye should have fellowship with devils.

GREEK WORDS

1. "taken"— **μ** (*lambano*): to seize; to attack; to grip; to take hold of

2. "common to man"— ϖ (*anthropinos*): anything experienced by human beings; unexceptional; merely human

3. "tempted"— ϖ μ (*peirasmos*): pictures an intense examination; a fiery trial or experience

4. "escape"— (*ekbasis*): to walk out, as to walk out of a difficult place; to walk away; to remove yourself from a person or place that isn't good for you; to use your feet to exit a situation or environment

5. "flee"— (*pheugo*): to run as fast as possible; to escape; to use one's feet to move as fast as possible to get out of an unprofitable situation; it is the picture of one's feet "flying" as he runs from a situation

SYNOPSIS

In these five lessons, Rick examines specific areas in which resistance to evil is required to live victoriously. You will discover biblical and practical wisdom on how to resist *temptation* and a *bad environment*; why it's necessary to resist the *faithless opinions* of others; and what steps to take to resist the *devil himself* and the *evil attacks* he brings. If you will hear and obey the Lord's instructions, you will be empowered to resist every evil temptation and trick that comes your way. In Christ, you are more than a conqueror!

The emphasis of this lesson:

God will make a way for you to escape *every* temptation you face!

All over the Greek and Roman world, there were pagan temples devoted to the worship of false gods. The Temple of Aphrodite, dedicated to the goddess of sex, is a perfect example. In this particular place of decadence, located in the city of Corinth, horrible acts of sexual debauchery and demonic activity took place. Ironically, temples were also marketplaces for the best cuts of meat in town. To purchase meat, believers had to expose themselves to the sights and sounds of sin — the sin in which many of them had once participated. These were places where believers didn't need to be.

Writing to the Corinthian believers, and ultimately to all believers, the apostle Paul said, "There hath no temptation taken you but such as is common to man: but God is faithful, who will not suffer you to be tempted above that ye are able; but will with the temptation also make a way to *escape...*" (1 Corinthians 10:13).

What It Means To 'Escape'

The word "escape" is the Greek word *ekbasis*, and it means *to get up, use your feet, and remove yourself from a person or place that isn't good for you.* Just as simply as you walked into a place, you can walk out of it. God has made a way for you to escape temptation using your own two feet! In fact, He says we are to "flee" temptation, which means *to move your feet as fast as you can and get out of there!* Don't stand around and allow yourself to become mesmerized or paralyzed by temptation. And don't believe the lie that you need to stick around in order to prove how spiritually strong you are. If you know something evil is trying to suck you in, get up and get moving before it traps you!

What are you resisting today? Is it gossip? Gluttony? Bitterness? Lust? Whatever it is, you are not alone. There is no temptation that is not "common to man" — temptation is simply part of the human experience.

Thankfully, all temptation can be conquered through the wisdom and strength of Christ!

If there are certain people you've been spending time with that fuel the fire of your temptation, *stop hanging out with them*. If they are instrumental in leading you away from God and into sin, *find some new friends*. Often you have to get very practical about the way you deal with temptation. For example, if porn is a problem for you — as it is for many men and even some women — put a filter on your computer and find someone you can be accountable to. Practical solutions can go a long way to help you avoid the pitfalls of temptation and sin.

Avoid the Scenes of Temptation

For believers living in Corinth, Paul gave the practical solution not to eat meat sacrificed to idols. The problem was not the meat. The real issue was the environment believers were subjecting themselves to in order to buy the meat. By going to pagan temples ripe with sexual immorality and demonic activity, they were putting themselves in jeopardy of being lured back into sin. Paul went so far as to say, "…I would not that ye should have *fellowship* with devils" (1 Corinthians 10:20). The word "fellowship" (*koinonia*), normally used to describe healthy interaction between believers, as well as with the Holy Spirit, was used here to describe unhealthy *participation and fellowship with demons*. If such a practice was not possible, Paul would not have warned against it.

Paul's message was an admonition to avoid the scenes of temptation!

God wants you to build your life in such a way that you *avoid* places of temptation. Referring to sexual temptation, He said, "Let your way in life be far from her, and come not near the door of her house [avoid the very scenes of temptation]" (Proverbs 5:8 *AMPC*). If you find yourself in a place (or with a person) that presents a tempting opportunity, look for the way of "escape." That is, look for the *exit* from that situation.

Lightning bolts and angelic appearances are not likely to occur to warn you and show you the way out — nor are they necessary to keep you from sinning. Just pray and reach for a practical, common-sense solution. The answer may be as simple as putting space between you and the place where sin has ruled and temptation now lurks to draw you back into sin and bondage.

God will make a way for you to escape *every* temptation you face!

STUDY QUESTIONS

Study to shew thyself approved unto God, a workman that needeth
not to be ashamed, rightly dividing the word of truth.
— 2 Timothy 2:15

1. In this life we will be tempted. Therefore, we must learn how to *resist* temptation so that we don't give in to sin. According to First Corinthians 10:13 and 14, what has God promised to provide you in every situation of temptation? How should you always respond to the lure of sexual sin?

2. In First Corinthians 10:19-21, the apostle Paul instructed believers not to eat meat sacrificed to idols. What was his real purpose in giving them this command? How can you apply this wisdom in your own life? (*See* Proverbs 4:25-27; 5:8; 1 Thessalonians 5:21, 22.)

3. The enemy's aim is to trap us in patterns of sin that keep us from growing spiritually, moving forward in our relationship with God, and fulfilling His plan for our lives. Is there a temptation you seem to keep giving in to? Where in your thoughts, words, or actions are you repeatedly tripped up?

PRACTICAL APPLICATION

But be ye doers of the word, and not hearers only,
deceiving your own selves.
— James 1:22

1. Rick shared how he was vulnerable to the temptation of eating certain unhealthy foods. Since that temptation came against him at a predictable time and place, he learned to *build his life* in such a way to avoid it. Knowing the temptations that regularly come against you, what are some practical "building" steps you can take in your own life to avoid falling into sin?

2. Proverbs 27:17 (*NLT*) says, "As iron sharpens iron, so a friend sharpens a friend." Having a friend — one who *knows* you and *loves* you — can be a great ally in your fight against temptation. Who genuinely wants to see you grow and become all God has called you to be? This person is a great candidate to be your accountability partner. How can you begin to connect with this individual regularly?

TOPIC

Resisting a Bad Environment

SCRIPTURES

1. **Hebrews 12:1** — Wherefore seeing we also are compassed about with
so great a cloud of witnesses, let us lay aside every weight, and the sin
which doth so easily beset us, and let us run with patience the race
that is set before us.

GREEK WORDS

1. "lay aside" — ϖ μ (*apotithemi*): to lay something down and
push it beyond reach so that it cannot be easily retrieved; a deliberate
decision to make a permanent change of attitude and behavior; can be
used to denote the removal of clothes

2. "weight" — (*ogkos*): a burden so heavy and cumbersome that it
impedes a runner from successfully running his race

3. "sin" — μ (*hamartia*): to miss the mark; a failure; a fault

4. "easily beset us" — ϖ (*euperistatos*): pictures something
that comfortably stands all around; a familiar environment that encircles a person's life; to environ

5. "run" — (*trecho*): pictures one who has jumped into the race
and is pressing ahead with all his might to reach a goal set before him;
one running at such a pace that both feet never hit the ground at the
same time; with eyes fixed on the finish line, the runner makes a dash
for it, steadily moving forward toward the goal

6. "race" — (*agon*): refers to athletic conflicts and competitions
that were famous in the ancient world; pictures wrestlers in a wres-
tling match, with each wrestler struggling with all his might to overcome his opponent in an effort to hurl him to the ground in a fight to
the finish; used figuratively to describe a struggle of the human will

SYNOPSIS

In the ancient city of Pergamum during the First Century, theatrical performances were observed in two big theaters, one of which was the Upper Theater. Nearly ten thousand people would gather at each performance, which featured a pre-show sacrifice to the "god" Dionysus. Drunken priests would walk an animal to the front of the stage and then take it to the temple of Dionysus in the distance and offer it on an altar. When the people in attendance saw the smoke billowing into the sky, they knew a sacrifice had been made, the gods were then appeased, and the show could begin.

For a Christian living in the First Century, these sacrificial rites were extremely disgusting and vile. Yet ordinary people had become accustomed to that type of behavior as part of their everyday culture. Today we are faced with a similar situation. The airwaves and the Internet are saturated with some of the vilest and most corrupt "entertainment" ever seen. The question is, what do we do with it? Do we accept what our culture and the courts tell us is normal, or do we live by a different standard?

The emphasis of this lesson:

If we want to make a change in our lives, we have to get involved and take action.

Learn To Resist Bad Environments

As believers, we are called to live by the standard of Scripture. Regardless of what the culture around us dictates, the Word of God — not society — determines our values of right and wrong, and we must choose to live by those values.

Believers in the First Century were surrounded by bad environments. The theater with its vulgarity, the pagan temples rife with demonic activity, and the bathhouses that hosted sexual immorality are all examples. Temptation abounded in these places, so Christians had to devise practical ways to build barriers between themselves and the negative influences around them. *They learned to resist those bad environments.*

Hebrews 12:1 says, "Wherefore seeing we also are compassed about with so great a cloud of witnesses, let us lay aside every weight, and the sin which doth so easily beset us, and let us run with patience the race that is set before us." The phrase "lay aside" is the Greek word *apotithemi*, and it means *to lay something down and push it beyond reach so that it cannot be easily retrieved.*

This is not something that happens automatically. It is *a deliberate decision to make a permanent change of attitude and behavior.* By using the word *apotithemi*, the writer of Hebrews is telling us, "If we want to make a change in our lives, we have to get involved and take action."

Identify the *Weights* and *Sin* That Slow You Down Personally

There are all kinds of things that negatively affect us and can hinder us from living a godly life. Specifically, God says to lay aside every "weight" — the Greek word *ogkos.* This signifies *anything cumbersome and heavy that is slowing us down in our walk with Him.* This includes unhealthy relationships, crippling spending habits, and harmful entertainment choices.

God also instructs us to lay aside any "sin" we're tolerating in our lives. "Sin," the word *hamartia*, indicates anything causing us *to fail to hit the mark of God's standard.* In both cases, God wants us to actively get involved and work at disentangling ourselves from such things.

The writer of Hebrews then further qualified the words "weight" and "sin" with the phrase "easily beset us." This phrase is translated from the Greek word *euperistatos*, and it describes *something that comfortably stands all around* or *a familiar environment that encircles* a person's life. This pictures something (or someone) we've been around so long and have become so accustomed to that we feel at home with this besetting situation. Yet as comfortable as we have become with it, it is negatively impacting our life and causing us to stumble and experience failure in our walk with God.

Whatever person, place, or thing you're tolerating that is dragging you down, it's not worth the sacrifice of missing out on God's will and purpose for your life. He wants you to begin the process of shedding any negative influence and of pressing toward the higher calling (*see* Philippians 3:13, 14). First-century believers had to make a conscious decision to avoid the bad environments that would corrupt their character, *and so must you.*

Run Your God-Appointed Race!

Once we recognize and lay aside the *weights* and the *sins* that are besetting us, we are to "run" (*trecho*) our "race" (*agon*). The word "run" pictures *one who has jumped into the race and is pressing ahead with all his might to reach a goal set before him.* He runs at such a pace that *both feet never hit the ground at the same time*! His eyes are fixed on *the finish line as he makes a mad dash for it, steadily moving toward the goal.*

The Greek word for "race" — *agon* — is where we get the term *agony.* It refers to *an athletic conflict or competition in which wrestlers were struggling with all their might to overcome their opponent.* Figuratively, it pictures *the intense struggle of the human will in a fight to the finish.* This tells us that when we get involved with our own life and future, it may be a struggle to remove ourselves from bad environments. Therefore, we have to be mentally prepared to stick with the decision we know is right. It will not be easy as we wrestle to "pin to the mat" any wayward part of our soul that is tempted by weights and sins. And we may not be able to do it immediately. Nevertheless, we must begin the process.

The Holy Spirit will show you what to disentangle from and how to do it. As you fix your eyes on Jesus, He will help you run your race at the proper pace energized by His grace. Now is the time to begin removing yourself from all that weighs you down, all that's causing you to fail, and all that contaminates your character. It's a new day, and there are new people, places, and things waiting for you to win!

STUDY QUESTIONS

Study to shew thyself approved unto God, a workman that needeth not to be ashamed, rightly dividing the word of truth.
— 2 Timothy 2:15

1. Scripture is full of examples of people who were hindered from moving forward in their relationship with God. Check out these passages concerning Lot's wife (Genesis 19:16-26) and the rich young ruler (Matthew 19:16-26). Identify the *weight* that slowed them down and the *wisdom* you can gain from their stories to apply to your own life.

2. Moses' life exemplifies what it means to "lay aside" something that stands all around you — an environment in which you feel very comfortable and at home (*euperistatos*). What was it that he laid aside to pursue the calling God had given him? (*See* Hebrews 11:24-27.) What does his example speak to you personally at your present age and stage of life?

3. The friends you spend time with regularly have a powerful impact on your life. The Bible confirms this again and again. Carefully read Proverbs 13:20 and 22:24, 25; First Corinthians 15:33; and Second Corinthians 6:14-18. What is the Lord showing you in these verses? What is He speaking to you about the people you hang out with regularly? What action is He prompting you to take regarding your relationships?

PRACTICAL APPLICATION

But be ye doers of the word, and not hearers only,
deceiving your own selves.
—James 1:22

1. In Hebrews 12:1, we are instructed to "lay aside every *weight*, and the *sin* which doth so easily beset us." A weight is not necessarily a sin; it is simply anything that is heavy and is weighing us down. What in your life is weighing you down? What types of attitudes or actions — or people, places, or things — are keeping you from effectively moving forward in your walk with God?

2. Are there any *besetting* sins in which you find yourself easily entangled? Is there a bad environment in which you have become comfortable? Take a few moments and describe what comes to mind.

3. In light of your answers to questions 1 and 2, what practical steps do you feel the Holy Spirit prompting you to take to become disentangled from these things and to lay them aside?

LESSON 3

TOPIC

Resisting Faithless Opinions

SCRIPTURES

1. **Hebrews 10:32, 33** — But call to remembrance the former days, in which, after ye were illuminated, ye endured a great fight of afflictions. Partly, whilst ye were made a gazingstock both by reproaches and afflictions; and partly, whilst ye became companions of them that were so used.

2. **1 Corinthians 4:9** — For I think that God hath set forth us the apostles last, as it were appointed to death: for we are made a spectacle unto the world, and to angels, and to men.

3. **1 Corinthians 4:13** — Being defamed, we intreat: we are made as the filth of the world, and are the offscouring of all things unto this day.

GREEK WORDS

1. "illuminated" — (*photidzo*): to illuminate; gives the impression of a brilliant flash of light that leaves a permanent and lasting impression

2. "endured" — μ (*meno*): to stay or abide; to resolve to maintain territory that has been gained; in a military sense, it pictures soldiers who were ordered to maintain their positions even in the face of fierce combat; to defiantly stick it out regardless of the pressure mounted against it; staying power; "hang-in-there" power; the attitude that holds out, holds on, outlasts, and perseveres, never giving up, refusing to surrender to obstacles, and turning down every opportunity to quit; pictures one who refuses to bend, break, or surrender because he is convinced that the territory, promise, or principle under assault rightfully belongs to him

3. "fight" — (*athlesis*): an athletic term that refers to the attitude and activities of a committed athlete; denotes athletic competitions or athletic games; can be translated as the word "struggle"; can denote a heroic act

4. "afflictions" — ϖ μ (*pathema*): a strong emotional struggle; emotional or mental agony; suffering

5. "gazingstock" — (*theatridzo*): a spectacle; to observe, to watch, to study, to scrutinize, or to bring upon a stage for all to see; also pictures spectators in a theater watching a scenario being played before them as they are on the edge of their seats; these spectators wait for actors to make a mistake or forget a line so they can scorn, ridicule, and make fun of them; can be interpreted as bringing onstage in order to scorn, scoff at, sneer at, shame, or publicly humiliate

SYNOPSIS

Like all theaters in major cities of the Roman world, the theater in the ancient city of Aphrodisias in the Roman province of Asia was a place where people were disdained and mocked. Those who took to the stage used that opportunity to mock and ridicule politicians and people they despised. Christians were often dragged onto the platform and made the laughing-stock of all who were present. As a spectacle of scorn, they were belittled and humiliated for their faith and their decision to follow Christ.

The writer of Hebrews refers to this in Hebrews 10:32, 33: "But call to remembrance the former days, in which, after ye were illuminated, ye endured a great fight of afflictions. Partly, whilst ye were made a gazingstock both by reproaches and afflictions; and partly, whilst ye became companions of them that were so used."

The word "gazingstock" is from the Greek word *theatridzo* from which we derive the word "theater." It depicts *a spectacle to observe, to watch, to study, to scrutinize, or to bring upon a stage for all to see.* It can also picture *spectators in a theater watching a scene being played before them as they sit on the edge of their seats.* These spectators wait for actors to make a mistake or forget a line so they can scorn, ridicule, and make fun of them. "Gazingstock" can also be interpreted to mean *bringing someone on a stage in order to scorn, scoff at, sneer at, shame, or publicly humiliate.* Indeed, early Christians became a "gazingstock" in the world in which they lived.

The emphasis of this lesson:

If you know you've been illuminated by the Spirit of God, make the decision to turn a deaf ear to all other voices, and focus on what He has told you to do.

Remember the Spiritual Milestones in Your Life

God wanted believers to "call to remembrance the former days." The phrase "call to remembrance" depicts *digging something up out of a grave, dusting it off, and looking at it again.* What did God want them to deliberately recall from memory? It was the "former days" in which they were "illuminated." The word "illuminated" is from the Greek word *photidzo*, and it's where we get the word *photo* or *photograph.* It means *to illuminate,* and it gives the impression of *a brilliant flash of light that leaves a permanent and lasting impression.*

A person is "illuminated" when he or she experiences a powerful revelation of truth — something so strong, so life-changing, that it leaves *a permanent, lasting impression* on the person's life. This includes the moment one hears the Gospel for the first time and humbly turns in repentance to Christ. It involves receiving eye-opening revelations about topics such as divine healing, the baptism in the Holy Spirit, the empowerment of God's grace, as well as discovering our divine calling and purpose. Like *a brilliant flash of light*, these moments of illumination become milestones in our walk with God that forever change our life.

This passage in Hebrews 10 says that with illumination comes "a great fight of afflictions." The word "great" signifies *many* or *manifold*. The word "fight" (*athlesis*) is an athletic term that refers to *the attitude and activities of a committed athlete*. It refers to athletic competitions or games that involve *intense struggle*.

This leads us to the word "afflictions" — the Greek word *pathema*, which indicates *a strong emotional or mental struggle of agony or suffering*. All these words taken together let us know that once we have been "illuminated," we'd better get ready for a fight!

Ignore the Naysayers and Maintain Your Post!

Like a professional athlete who takes every match seriously, *you* must make a decision to resist the enemy — especially in the arenas of your mind and emotions. The same devil who was against the advancement of the Kingdom of God in the first centuries is against the advancement of God's Kingdom today. The enemy will do everything he can to orchestrate his attacks, including using faithless opinions through the mouths of others to discourage and defeat you. Resisting Satan and circumstances can be challenging — but the *greatest* challenge you will face at times is resisting the faithless opinions of others, especially of people you know.

Sometimes the best way to deal with the harsh things people say in ignorance is to simply *ignore* them. The truth is, if you listen to your critics — who will sometimes include your family and friends — instead of listening to the Lord, they may derail you from your God-ordained destiny. If you know you've been illuminated by the Spirit of God, make the decision to turn a deaf ear to all other voices and focus on what He has told you to do.

We are called to "endure" afflictions — from the Greek word *meno*. In a military sense, this word depicted soldiers who were ordered to maintain their position even in the face of fierce combat. "Endure" in Hebrews 10:32 means *to stay or abide; to defiantly stick it out, regardless of the pressure mounted against it; staying power; "hang-in-there" power; the attitude that holds out, holds on, outlasts, perseveres, and never gives up.* As believers, we have to make a decision to maintain the territory God has given us, holding tenaciously to what God has shown us.

So whenever you are "illuminated" by the Lord and choose to follow Him, walking in the light of what He reveals to you, know in advance that you may be made a laughingstock by others. Sadly, even some immature Christians will join in the jabs, looking and laughing at you when you hear a word from God and begin to step out in obedience to fulfill it.

But regardless of the ridicule or rejection, never forget the milestones of God moving in your life! They are priceless treasures worth "calling to remembrance" — digging up, dusting off, and enjoying once again (*see* Hebrews 10:32). The psalmist echoed this directive saying, "I will remember the works of the Lord: surely I will remember thy wonders of old. I will meditate also of all thy work, and talk of thy doings" (Psalm 77:11, 12).

Choose to ignore the *faithless opinions* of others. Set your face like flint (*see* Isaiah 50:7) to have what God said you can have and do what He said you can do. He has promised to be with you and to help you. Through the abiding power of His Spirit, you can endure any affliction that comes your way. Like a soldier at his post, you can unflinchingly choose to stay where God told you to stay and do what He told you to do. In Christ, you are a history maker!

STUDY QUESTIONS

Study to shew thyself approved unto God, a workman that needeth not to be ashamed, rightly dividing the word of truth.
— 2 Timothy 2:15

1. The word "illuminated" (*photidzo*) means *to illuminate something so strongly that it leaves a lasting, permanent impression.* It's like taking a high-resolution photograph of something you will never forget. Take a moment and reflect on when you were first "illuminated" by the Lord. Dust off that experience and describe what hearing the Gospel message for the first time was like. How did you feel inside when you invited Christ into your life?

2. Why is the devil afraid of our receiving a word from God and becoming "illuminated"? What does he know will happen that we often forget in the midst of the fiery afflictions he tries to bring our way?

3. Think about the many men and women in Scripture who heard God's calling, chose to follow Him, and were made a "gazingstock" or spectacle of ridicule and humiliation. What biblical character do you admire most who found himself or herself in this exact position? Explain why this person's story inspires you.

PRACTICAL APPLICATION

But be ye doers of the word, and not hearers only,
deceiving your own selves.
—James 1:22

1. Name a major spiritual milestone in your life in which the Lord powerfully revealed something to you that left a permanent, lasting change on your life (e.g., insight about your spouse, children, career, God's character, etc.). How did this illumination positively impact those around you?

2. Interestingly, the people who have the strongest negative opinion about your stepping out to do what God has told you to do are usually those who have never done anything with the call of God on their own lives. Why do you think this is the case? Who should you be listening to for wisdom and direction in your endeavors? Why?

3. When you're being "defamed" with words of shame and ridicule, God wants you to receive encouragement from others. Who are you doing life with that can provide such comfort and encouragement? Who do you know who could really use some words of encouragement right now? Take some time to reach out and be a source of strength to them (*see* Galatians 6:10).

LESSON 4

TOPIC
Resisting the Devil

SCRIPTURES

1. **James 4:7** — Submit yourselves therefore to God. Resist the devil, and he will flee from you.

2. **1 Peter 5:8, 9** — Be sober, be vigilant; because your adversary the devil, as a roaring lion, walketh about, seeking whom he may devour: whom resist stedfast in the faith, knowing that the same afflictions are accomplished in your brethren that are in the world.

3. **John 10:10** — The thief cometh not, but for to steal, and to kill, and to destroy: I am come that they might have life, and that they might have it more abundantly.

4. **2 Timothy 4:13** — The cloke that I left at Troas with Carpus, when thou comest, bring with thee, and the books, but especially the parchments.

5. **Hebrews 10:25** — Not forsaking the assembling of ourselves together, as the manner of some is; but exhorting one another: and so much more, as ye see the day approaching.

6. **Psalm 119:164, 165** — Seven times a day do I praise thee because of thy righteous judgments. Great peace have they which love thy law: and nothing shall offend them.

7. **James 5:12** — But above all things, my brethren, swear not, neither by heaven, neither by earth, neither by any other oath: but let your yea be yea; and your nay, nay; lest ye fall into condemnation.

8. **Ephesians 5:18** — And be not drunk with wine, wherein is excess; but be filled with the Spirit.

GREEK WORDS

1. "vigilant" — (*gregoreo*): be on your guard; be alert; be aware

2. "adversary" — (*antidikos*): a prosecutor; a lawyer; one who prosecutes

3. "devil" — (*diabolos*): one who repetitiously strikes until successfully penetrating an object in order to ruin it or take it captive; to slander, accuse, or defame; to penetrate by continuous assault

4. "devour" — ω (*pino*): to drink; to consume; to devour; to slurp

5. "thief" — ω (*kleptes*): a bandit, thief, or scam artist

6. "steal" — ω (*klepto*): one so artful in the way he steals that his exploits of thievery are nearly undetectable; a pickpocket; it is where we get the word "kleptomaniac"

7. "kill" — (*thuo*): not kill, as in murder, but to sacrifice; to surrender or give up something that is precious and dear

8. "destroy" — ϖ μ (*apollumi*): to ruin, waste, trash, devastate, or destroy

9. "life" — (*zoe*): life filled with vitality

10. "abundantly" — ϖ (*perissos*): excessively; exceedingly; extraordinarily; something that abounds in an extraordinary measure; something so profuse that it can be likened to a river spilling over and flooding its banks; overflowing, plentiful, or even superabundant

11. "resist" — μ (*anthistemi*): to resist; to arrange oneself against; to strategically oppose; an orderly and planned resistance

12. "stedfast" — (*stereos*): to bolster; to reinforce

SYNOPSIS

The Altar of Zeus, located in the ancient city of Pergamum, was very prominent in the city due to its intricate architectural design. Even in ancient times, it was so massive and magnificent that it was deemed one of the Seven Wonders of the Ancient World. Yet it was spiritually one of the darkest places in all of Asia. In Revelation 2:13, Jesus Himself referred to it as "Satan's seat." It was a place of deep, dark, concentrated demonic power. This was true of almost the entire city of Pergamum. But it was to this city that God called believers to build His Church. And it became a place where they needed to learn how to live for Him despite the trappings of their dark, evil surroundings.

James 4:7 says, "Submit yourselves therefore to God. Resist the devil, and he will flee from you." Many Christians who lived in Pergamum learned how to resist the devil. They knew how to recognize his voice and his methods of operation and to stand effectively against him. As a result, the enemy did indeed flee from a group of consecrated believers who held fast to Christ's name.

The emphasis of this lesson:

The devil is a defeated foe, but we must learn how to reinforce his defeat and to live in Christ's victory in our everyday lives.

Understand the Devil's Methods

First Peter 5:8 says, "Be sober, be vigilant; because your adversary the devil, as a roaring lion, walketh about, seeking whom he may devour."

The word "vigilant" is the Greek word *gregoreo,* which means *to be on your guard; be alert; be aware.* At all times, we must be aware that the enemy is trying to find an entryway into our lives. Therefore we must live *alert* and *on guard* and learn to recognize the methods of our "adversary." This word, from the Greek word *antidikos,* means *a prosecutor, a lawyer, or one who prosecutes.*

Satan is very sly in his operations, bringing thoughts of slander and false accusation against you. He will try to prosecute and imprison you using information he knows about your past actions and present struggles. But remember, he is a liar and there is no truth in him (*see* John 8:44).

Next in First Peter 5:8, Peter used the word "devil" — from the Greek word *diabolos* — indicating *one who repetitiously strikes until successfully penetrating an object in order to ruin it or take it captive.*

Diabolos also means *to slander, accuse,* or *defame,* or *to penetrate by continuous assault.* The word *diabolos* is really more Satan's job description than his name. He strikes again and again with one lie after another — for the sole purpose of penetrating our minds and destroying our lives.

He is seeking "whom he may devour," which lets us know that not everyone can be devoured. The devil is looking for loners, stragglers, and those who are spiritually weak. These are his prime targets. "Devour" is from the Greek word *pino,* and it means *to drink, to consume, to devour,* or *to slurp.* Satan doesn't just want to attack you; he wants to totally pummel, slaughter, and consume your life — as a lion does its prey — so that there's no "meat left on the bone." This word "devour" paints a picture of him *slurping* up the last drops of blood that remain.

Comprehending the Vile Character of the Thief

Jesus said in John 10:10, "The thief cometh not but for to steal, and to kill, and to destroy: I am come that they might have life, and that they might have it more abundantly." The word for "thief" is *kleptes,* and it describes *a bandit, thief,* or *scam artist.*

Satan — the thief — is very slick in his acts of thievery. The first thing Jesus said he does is "to *steal*" — the Greek word *klepto.* This word pictures *a pickpocket* and *one so artful in the way he steals that his exploits of thievery are nearly undetectable. Klepto* is where we get the word "kleptomaniac."

Satan is a pickpocketing, kleptomaniac scam artist whose *entire character* is bent on stealing.

The second thing Jesus said the thief comes to do is "to *kill*," from the Greek word *thuo*. This word "kill" does not mean murder at all. Instead, it literally means *to sacrifice* — and it specifically refers to *a religious sacrifice*.

"To kill" carries the meaning of *surrendering or giving up something that is precious and dear*. In other words, once the adversary has robbed someone blind, he disguises his voice and tries to talk that person into believing he needs to sacrifice everything else in his life that's good. He comes with a voice of reason and logic, sometimes even sounding like God, to get that person to sacrifice everything he holds precious and dear. That thief will take whatever someone is willing to let him have — whether it be that person's joy, peace, health, marriage, family relationships, job — you name it.

Third, Jesus said the thief moves in to "destroy" whatever remains in a person's life. "Destroy" — the Greek word *apollumi* — means *to undo* or *to ruin, waste, trash, devastate, or destroy*.

Putting the meanings of all these words together, here is the *Renner Interpretive Version* (*RIV*) for the first part of John 10:10:

> **The thief wants to get his hands into every good thing in your life. In fact, this pickpocket is looking for any opportunity to wiggle his way so deeply into your personal affairs that he can walk off with everything you hold precious and dear.**
>
> **And that's not all — when he's finished stealing all your goods and possessions, he'll take his plan to rob you blind to the next level by creating conditions and situations so horrible that you'll see no way to solve the problems except to sacrifice everything that remains from previous attacks.**
>
> **The goal of this thief is to totally devastate your life. If nothing stops him, he'll leave you insolvent, flat broke, and cleaned out in every area of your life. You'll end up feeling as if you are finished and out of business! Make no mistake — the enemy's ultimate aim is to obliterate you.**

Seven Things To Do Every Day To Make Yourself Strong and To *Resist Evil*

First Peter 5:9 tells us we are to "resist" the enemy and to be "stedfast in the faith." The word "resist" is the Greek word *anthistemi*, which means *to resist; to arrange oneself against;* or *to strategically oppose.* It pictures *an orderly and planned resistance.* The word "stedfast" is the Greek word *stereos,* which means *to bolster or reinforce yourself* against attack.

The following are seven things you can do every day to ensure you remain spiritually strong in the Lord so you can resist every evil temptation, trap, and attack of the enemy.

1. **Every day spend time with God in the morning.** (*See* Psalm 5:1-3 and 27:4.)

2. **Every day spend time feeding your spirit on God's Word and other godly sources.** (*See* Jeremiah 15:16; Hebrews 4:12; 2 Timothy 3:16, 17; 4:13.)

3. **Every day spend some time in quietness.** (*See* Psalm 46:10 and 62:1, 2, 5, 6.)

4. **Every day spend some time with people who strengthen you.** (*See* Proverbs 27:17; Hebrews 10:25.)

5. **Every day take time throughout the day to acknowledge God.** (*See* Psalm 119:164, 165.)

6. **Every day say no to the things you are not supposed to do.** (*See* James 5:12.)

7. **Every day pray to be filled with the Holy Spirit anew.** (*See* Ephesians 5:18.)

STUDY QUESTIONS

> Study to shew thyself approved unto God, a workman that needeth
> not to be ashamed, rightly dividing the word of truth.
> — 2 Timothy 2:15

1. The word "devil" (*diabolos*) is more of a job description than a name. How does the Greek meaning of this word help you better understand the difficulties you have perhaps been facing? How does it encourage you and help you see things more accurately in your resisting the enemy?

2. According to First Peter 5:8, the devil cannot devour just anyone. There are only certain people he's able to overcome. Who is the enemy seeking? What makes these people vulnerable to his attacks? What can you do to be more "vigilant" and to guard yourself from being his victim?

3. The Word of God clearly says that you have power over the enemy! Look up these promises in Scripture — Luke 10:19; Colossians 2:15; Isaiah 54:17; 1 John 4:4 — and write out and commit to memory the verse that energizes you most.

PRACTICAL APPLICATION

But be ye doers of the word, and not hearers only, deceiving your own selves.
— James 1:22

1. The devil is referred to in Scripture as our "adversary" (*antidikos*), which means he is *a prosecutor or lawyer* who comes against us with one twisted charge after another in an attempt to "put us away" in his prison. Take a moment and identify the voice of the "adversary" in your life. Describe some of the specific accusations he has been bringing against *you*. Then, using a Bible concordance, look up specific words of truth from your Defense Attorney, Jesus Christ — words to combat and crush Satan's accusing lies. (Consider these verses: Romans 5:6-8 and 8:1, 2, 31-39; 2 Corinthians 5:17, 21; Ephesians 1:3-8; 1 John 3:1, 2.)

2. Jesus said that Satan — the thief — comes to *steal, kill*, and *destroy*. Carefully reread the *Renner Interpretive Version* (*RIV*) of John 10:10. How does this expanded meaning help you better see how the enemy has been operating in your life? How does it motivate you to stand against him?

3. Take a few minutes to read over "Seven Things To Do Every Day To Make Yourself Strong and To *Resist Evil.*" Which of these things are you presently doing? Can you think of ways you can "come up higher" in the way you practice these behaviors systematically? Pause for a moment and pray: "Lord, what adjustments do I need to make in my daily routine to better incorporate these seven habits in my life?" Be still and listen. What is the Holy Spirit showing you?

TOPIC

Resisting Evil Attacks

SCRIPTURES

1. **1 Corinthians 10:13, 14** — There hath no temptation taken you but such as is common to man: but God is faithful, who will not suffer you to be tempted above that ye are able; but will with the temptation also make a way to escape, that ye may be able to bear it. Wherefore, my dearly beloved, flee from idolatry.

2. **Hebrews 12:1** — Wherefore seeing we also are compassed about with so great a cloud of witnesses, let us lay aside every weight, and the sin which doth so easily beset us, and let us run with patience the race that is set before us.

3. **Hebrews 10:32, 33** — But call to remembrance the former days, in which, after ye were illuminated, ye endured a great fight of afflictions. Partly, whilst ye were made a gazingstock both by reproaches and afflictions; and partly, whilst ye became companions of them that were so used.

4. **John 10:10** — The thief cometh not, but for to steal, and to kill, and to destroy: I am come that they might have life, and that they might have it more abundantly.

5. **James 4:7** — Submit yourselves therefore to God. Resist the devil, and he will flee from you.

GREEK WORDS

1. "common to man" — ω (*anthropinos*): commonplace to humans; a common human problem or trait that has already been faced and overcome by others in the past

2. "escape" — (*ekbasis*): to walk out, as to walk out of a difficult place; to step out; to walk out of a trap; the act of removing yourself from a place that isn't good for you; to walk out of or away from

3. "flee" — (*pheugo*): to flee; to run away; to run as fast as possible; to escape; pictures one's feet "flying" as he runs from a situation

4. "easily beset us" — ω (*euperistatos*): depicts something that comfortably stands all around; to easily and comfortably surround; pictures a familiar environment that encircles a person's life; to environ

5. "gazingstock" — (*theatridzo*): pictures bringing someone onto a stage for all to see; depicts spectators in a theater watching a scene being played before them; on the edge of their seats, these spectators wait for the actors to make a mistake or forget a line so they can scorn, ridicule, and make fun of them; can be interpreted as bringing onto to the stage in order to scorn, scoff at, shame, sneer at, and to publicly humiliate; a spectacle; it is where we get the word theater

6. "thief" — ω (*kleptes*): a bandit, thief, or scam artist

7. "steal" — ω (*klepto*): one so artful in the way he steals that his exploits of thievery are nearly undetectable; a pickpocket; it is where we get the word "kleptomaniac"

8. "kill" — (*thuo*): not kill, as in murder, but to sacrifice; to surrender or to give up something that is precious and dear

SYNOPSIS

Those who are sick are in search of healing. People living in the first and second centuries were no exception. The Asklepion, a massive medical treatment center, located in the upper part of ancient Pergamum, attracted sick people from all over the Roman world. They came for supernatural help. It was called the Asklepion because it was dedicated to the god Asklepios, the Greek god of healing.

As part of the healing process, the sick would sleep in certain rooms of the Asklepion facility. In the morning, the priests of Asklepios would interview the patients to find out what they had dreamed. Based on their dreams, the pagan priests would then prescribe the supernatural antidote required to heal them.

Interestingly, the serpent was the symbol of the god Asklepios. Accordingly, priests would release "sacred" snakes into the rooms where sick people slept. They believed if one of the snakes slithered across or touched a person's body, it was a sign that Asklepios was touching that person in a supernatural way. This was a very dark and evil religion — the kind of evil the Early Church had to know how to resist.

The emphasis of this lesson:

Before you can resist the enemy, you must *first* submit yourself to God.

Today we face many forms of evil that open the door for attacks on our lives. Addictions, sexual immorality, and warped political and moral philosophies affect the way we think as a society, and some of these mindsets have seeped into the Church. Our culture is constantly pushing the envelope, substituting worldly cures for God's prescribed answers that can be found in His Word. This morally altered society is throwing away timeless truths in exchange for ideas that don't line up with Scripture. What is the Church's responsibility and role in this hour — in the lives of individual believers and as the Church as a whole?

We are to *resist evil* as we take a strong stand on the truth of God's Word. We must demonstrate Christ's victory — and Satan's defeat — that was wrought in Christ's death, burial, and resurrection.

In the previous four lessons, we saw four kinds of evil we need to learn to resist:

- Resisting Temptation
- Resisting Faithless Opinions
- Resisting the Devil
- Resisting Bad Environments

Resist Temptation

Writing to the Corinthian believers, and ultimately to all believers, the apostle Paul said, "There hath no temptation taken you but such as is common to man: but God is faithful, who will not suffer you to be tempted above that ye are able; but will with the temptation also make a way to escape..." (1 Corinthians 10:13).

The phrase "common to man" is the Greek word *anthropinos*, which means *a common human problem or trait that has already been faced and overcome by others in the past.* This is important to keep in mind. The enemy would like you to think you are the *only one* going through the struggle you're in, but that is not true. If you look at your problem and *magnify* it, you'll only make it worse and reinforce its strength. However, if you *minimize* it by holding it up to the light of the truth, it will be easier to overcome.

Although God does not send problems to you, He will always make a way for you to *escape* them. This word "escape" in First Corinthians 10:13 is the

Greek word *ekbasis*, and it means *to walk out of a difficult place or trap* or *to walk out of or away from*. It also refers to *the act of removing yourself from a place that isn't good for you*. In other words, if you find yourself in a tough place of temptation, look for the way of escape. Then once you see it, *run!*

The very next verse, First Corinthians 10:14, says, "Wherefore, my beloved, *flee* from idolatry." The word "flee" means *to flee or run away from as fast as possible*. It is the picture of one's feet "flying" as he runs from a situation.

If you're facing temptation, the way to resist it is to move your feet as fast as you can and *flee*. God will make a way of escape, so *look* for the exit!

Resist Bad Environments

Hebrews 12:1 says, "Wherefore seeing we also are compassed about with so great a cloud of witnesses, let us lay aside every weight, and the sin which doth so easily beset us, and let us run with patience the race that is set before us." The phrase "easily beset" is the Greek word *euperistatos*, and it *depicts something that comfortably stands all around; a familiar environment that encircles a person's life*.

In the context of this verse, the environment is *bad*. It is a person, place, or thing with which you were once very comfortable, but is no longer good for you. It is weighing you down and hindering your spiritual progress. It may be an environment of drinking, gossiping, pride, legalism, unbelief, or sexual immorality. It is these types of environments that the Bible says to "lay aside."

Resist Faithless Opinions

In Hebrews 10:32 and 33, the writer said, "But call to remembrance the former days, in which, after ye were illuminated, ye endured a great fight of afflictions. Partly, whilst ye were made a gazingstock both by reproaches and afflictions; and partly, whilst ye became companions of them that were so used."

From this passage, we learn that once we have been "illuminated" about something, we are often thrown into a fight of afflictions, including a fight against the *faithless opinions* of others who don't agree with our illumination. The passage goes on to say we become a "gazingstock" to others. This term is from the Greek word *theatridzo*, meaning *to be brought on a stage for all to see.* It is the picture of *spectators in the theater watching a scenario being played before them.*

Strangely, we are the "show" people bought a ticket for to sit and watch. They wait for us to make a mistake so they can scorn, ridicule, and make fun of us.

Rather than become a victim of the faithless opinions of others, you need to surround yourself with people of faith who will love and support you. Turn a deaf ear to those who haven't done anything for God with their lives — but, rather, tune in to those who have done and are doing something with the illumination from God and His Word that they've received.

Resist the Devil

In Lesson 4, we learned how to resist the devil himself. In John 10:10, Jesus said, "The thief cometh not, but for to steal, and to kill, and to destroy: I am come that they might have life, and that they might have it more abundantly."

The word "thief" is the Greek word *kleptes* — the term from which we get the word "kleptomaniac." Essentially, Jesus said the devil is a *kleptomaniac* who is bent on taking everything he can from anyone who will let him. It has become inherent in his nature to do so.

When Satan — still known at that time as Lucifer — was in Heaven, he tried to take the worship and glory of God for himself. When he was in the Garden of Eden, he tried to take Adam's position of authority. Today Satan continues his thievery by attempting to steal our joy, our peace, our righteousness, and anything else he can get his hands on that doesn't belong to him.

First, Satan comes to "steal" — the Greek word *klepto*, which is the active form of *kleptes* (thief). This portion of the verse could be translated as follows: *When the kleptomaniac shows up, he'll start acting like a kleptomaniac. He'll try to clean you out, take you to the cleaners, and leave you flat broke. He is a pickpocket, a bandit, a kleptomaniac.*

Once Satan has robbed you blind, he will come to "kill" — the Greek word *thuo*, which describes *a religious sacrifice.* When Satan comes, he whispers thoughts that sound very religious. He sometimes even disguises his voice to sound like God. He'll say things like, *There's no hope of recovering. Everything has been lost. You should take whatever remains and offer it on the altar.*

Don't listen to him. He is a liar who comes to "steal, kill, and destroy." Learn to recognize and *resist* him!

Submit Yourself to God

James 4:7 tells us, "Submit yourselves therefore to God. Resist the devil, and he will flee from you." Before you can resist the enemy, you must *first* submit yourself to God. If you try to resist the devil in your own strength, he will soundly defeat you.

The word "submit" is a military term, which means *to fall in line and find yourself ordered under the authority of God*. Submitting yourself to God indicates that your spiritual life is in order. This includes repenting of any sin and making sure everything is right between you and Him. You are obeying His Word and submitted to His authority, which includes the authority He has placed over you.

In the position of submission to God, you can effectively resist the devil, and the Scripture says he will "flee." This is the same Greek word we looked at earlier — the word *pheugo*, which means *to move your feet as fast as you can and run away*. In other words, the devil won't just inch away from you when you resist him. He will move his feet as fast as he can and rush away from you in terror!

Don't let the devil push you around another day. Submit yourself to God and resist the devil and every evil temptation and attack he brings!

STUDY QUESTIONS

Study to shew thyself approved unto God, a workman that needeth not to be ashamed, rightly dividing the word of truth.
— 2 Timothy 2:15

1. Temptation is a part of life. Yet God has promised that with every temptation, He will make a way of escape (*see* 1 Corinthians 10:13). How else has He promised to help us when we're faced with temptation? Look up these additional promises in Hebrews 2:17, 18; 4:15, 16; and 2 Peter 2:9. What is the Holy Spirit showing you in these verses? How do they encourage you?

2. Submission to God is a powerful position and one that is required to effectively resist the devil and see him flee from you. The most diffi-

cult time to submit is when God tells you to do something that you don't understand or that your flesh doesn't like. Check out these two snapshots of submission — one concerning Mary (Luke 1:26-38) and the other concerning Jesus (Matthew 26:36-46). What do you see in these examples? What wisdom can you learn from them and apply to your own life?

PRACTICAL APPLICATION

**But be ye doers of the word, and not hearers only,
deceiving your own selves.
—James 1:22**

1. Briefly describe the greatest temptation you are faced with presently? Be honest. How are you looking at it? Are you *magnifying* its strength, believing it is too big to overcome and that you're the *only one* dealing with such an issue? Or are you *minimizing* its strength, knowing it is something common to all people and beatable with God's help? Give evidence to support your answer.

2. Sometimes God allows us to be in a certain environment for a season, and then when that season is up, He prompts us to move out of it. Is there a person, a place, or a thing that you once had no problem being connected with, but now you no longer have peace about? Maybe it's a group of friends, a source of entertainment, or an activity that is negatively impacting you. Take a moment and describe what the Holy Spirit is bringing to the surface of your mind. What action do you sense He wants you to take?

3. Have you been "illuminated" by God with fresh revelation, but have found yourself on the receiving end of the faithless opinions of others? If so, briefly describe the situation. Pause and pray, "Lord, how do You want me to respond in this situation? How can I be loving and respectful to these people and still hold tightly to what You have revealed?" Be still and listen for His reply. What is He instructing you to do?

www.ingramcontent.com/pod-product-compliance
Lightning Source LLC
Chambersburg PA
CBHW060558030426
42337CB00019B/3569